REAL REPERTOIRE LIBRARY

Real Repertoire
Studies
grades 6–8

Selected and edited by Christine Brown

FABER *ff* MUSIC

EDITOR'S NOTE

The *Real Repertoire Studies* series introduces players to a wealth of original works by the great writers of studies from Clementi to Bartók. They have been selected to give more advanced pianists a wide range of technical training in pieces which also provide musical interest. All could be played in festivals or concerts, many of them being ideal encores. Some additional fingering has been added to ensure consistency and some phrasing and pedalling marks have been clarified. The metronome marks without brackets are the composer's while those with brackets are editorial, but all should be treated with caution. Always practise the studies slowly at first then gradually increase the tempo over months or even years. I trust that these fine studies will bring much pleasure as well as great technical benefit to those who practise them.

Christine Brown

© 2008 by Faber Music Ltd
This edition first published in 2008
3 Queen Square London WC1N 3AU
Music processed by Jackie Leigh
Cover design by Sue Clarke
Printed in England by Caligraving Ltd
All rights reserved

ISBN10: 0-571-52605-5
EAN13: 978-0-571-52605-5

To buy Faber Music or Trinity publications or to find out about the full range of titles
available please contact your local music retailer or Faber Music sales enquiries:

Faber Music Ltd, Burnt Mill, Elizabeth Way, Harlow CM20 2HX
Tel: +44 (0)1279 82 89 82   Fax: +44 (0)1279 82 89 83
sales@fabermusic.com   fabermusic.com

THE COMPOSERS AND THEIR STUDIES

BÉLA BARTÓK (1881-1945) was born in Transylvania, then part of Hungary. Having shown early promise as a pianist and composer he entered the Liszt Academy in Budapest at the age of eighteen. Only eight years later he succeeded his own teacher Thoman as professor in charge of piano teaching. Bartók wrote the six volumes of *Mikrokosmos* to provide pianists with a course of training which would enable them to play music of the twentieth century. *Finger Study* is the ninth of ten pieces which Bartók wrote to supply his students at the Academy with short pieces in a contemporary style, so the five-finger patterns are based not on the usual major or minor scale patterns but on the two possible whole-tone scales. If the composer's fingering is observed the hands will learn these new shapes and be better prepared for twentieth century music.

JOHANN FRIEDRICH BURGMÜLLER (1806-1874) was born in Regensburg where his father was a music director and composer. In 1832 he settled in Paris and established himself as a pianist, teacher and composer before withdrawing from public life at the age of thirty-eight in order to concentrate on his teaching. His Studies Op. 100 and Op.109 have remained popular with pupils and teachers because they enable students to acquire valuable technical skills through practising attractive music. Burgmüller's original metronome speeds are given, but they should be considered an ultimate goal because much slower speeds will be necessary in the early stages. *Velocity* is an ideal study through which to develop speed in right-hand semiquavers. The left-hand chords should be carefully balanced and all articulation and dynamic indications should be observed to produce the finest effect.

MUZIO CLEMENTI (1752–1832) was born in Rome but spent most of his life in England. He became famous as a pianist, teacher, composer, publisher and piano manufacturer. His *Introduction to the Art of Playing on the Piano Forte* introduced many students to the newly-invented instrument while its supplement of the *Six Sonatinas* is still popular today. Although Clementi wrote much other music (including over a hundred piano sonatas) he is chiefly remembered for his *Gradus ad Parnassum*, three volumes of studies to enable pianists to develop the technique to play the music of the period. The studies employ every possible variety of keyboard figuration for each hand in turn in the context of a piece with musical as well as technical qualities. The *Study in A* is a good example with polyphonic interest to balance the scale, arpeggio and broken chord passage work. The *Study in F*, which concentrates on octave technique, should be practised slowly at first, always keeping the wrists loose.

JOHANN BAPTIST CRAMER (1771–1858) was born in Germany into a musical family who then moved to London. Having shown early promise as a pianist he became a pupil of Clementi and had a very successful career as a performer, composer and teacher. Indeed Beethoven was said to have considered him the finest pianist of the day (and he certainly helped to introduce Beethoven's Sonatas to audiences in England). His 84 studies entitled *Studio per il pianoforte* published in two sets, in 1804 and 1810, are still considered as having the utmost importance in helping pianists to acquire a well-developed technique, especially in regard to the equal development of the hands. In the *Study in F minor* the left hand must play the constant flow of semiquavers smoothly and with even tone, while the right hand phrases with care so that the expressive nature of the piece is captured. In the *Study in D major* the graceful arpeggios which are divided between the hands must sound as though played by one hand.

CARL CZERNY (1791–1857), the Austrian pianist, teacher and composer, was a pupil of Beethoven in his youth and later became known as one of the finest interpreters of his master's music. From an early age Czerny supported himself by teaching and among his pupils were Liszt, Thalberg and Kullak. He was a prolific composer, but his fame today rests on the large number of volumes of studies for the piano including his *School of Velocity*, Op.299 and *The Art of Finger Dexterity*, Op.740. Czerny had a remarkable understanding of piano technique and was able to devise a suitable study for any pupil who had a particular weakness. The *Study in D flat* prepares the left hand for the necessary flexibility in the playing of wide-ranging semiquaver passages and it requires careful balance between the hands. Practising the dramatic *Study in D minor* from *The Art of Finger Dexterity* will develop both strength and speed in the fingers of both hands.

THOMAS DUNHILL (1877–1946) studied piano and composition at the Royal College of Music and then became Assistant Music Master at Eton, also teaching harmony and counterpoint at the Royal College of Music. *The Wheel of Progress, Thirty Pianoforte Studies in Various Styles* is a valuable collection covering many aspects of piano technique. The final study, Book III, No.10 is excellent for developing the ability to play staccato sixths, an essential preparation for performing staccato octaves. It is vital to keep the wrist loose and to pay careful attention to the composer's own fingering for the maximum benefit from this enjoyable piece.

STEPHEN HELLER (1813-1888) was born in Hungary. He was a child prodigy and toured Europe with much success until his health was seriously affected. Eventually he settled in Paris and made a living as a pianist and composer. His short imaginative studies, written for musical rather than technical purposes, are still valued for their quality today. The *Etude in C* provides training for the playing of rapid octaves while the *Study in E* gives excellent practice in balancing a cantabile melody in both hands with a broken chord accompaniment in the right hand.

ALEXANDER NIKOLAYEVITCH SCRIABIN (1872–1915), equally gifted as a composer and as a pianist, studied at the Moscow Conservatory at the same time as Rachmaninov. The *Study in C sharp minor*, written in his early teens, is an astonishingly mature work showing the influence of Chopin combined with typically Russian melancholy. Separate hand practice will be required at first to gain the correct tonal balance between the parts within each hand and when the hands are played together much careful listening will be needed to obtain a good balance between all the parts.

VELOCITY

Op.109, No.10

Johann Friedrich Burgmüller
(1806–1874)

FINGER STUDY

from Ten Easy Piano Pieces

Béla Bartók
(1881–1945)

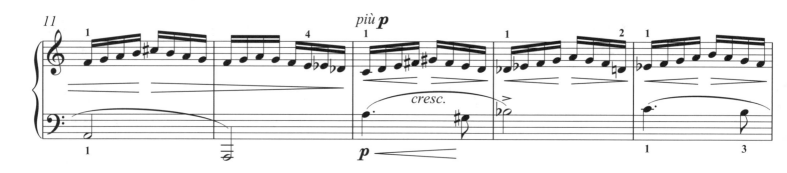

STUDY IN D
Op.30, No.33

Johann Baptist Cramer
(1771–1858)

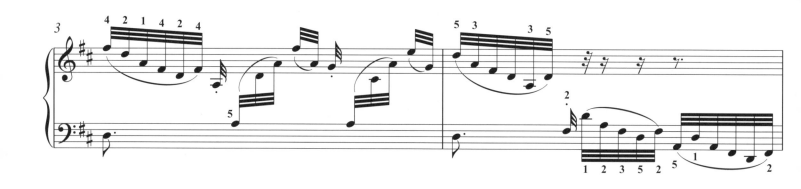

STUDY IN C

from The Wheel of Progress, Book III, No. 10

Thomas F. Dunhill
(1877–1946)

STUDY IN D FLAT

Op.636, No.18

Carl Czerny
(1791–1857)

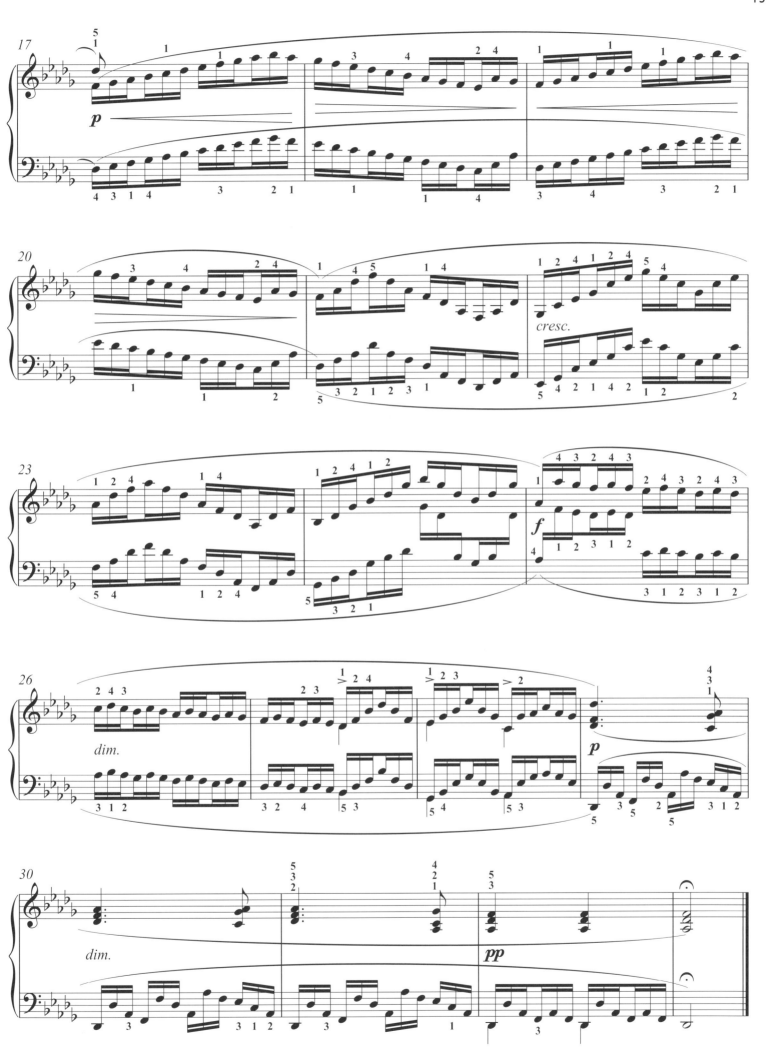

ETUDE IN C
Op.46, No.24

Stephen Heller
(1813–1888)

Allegro con brio (♩. = *c*.80)

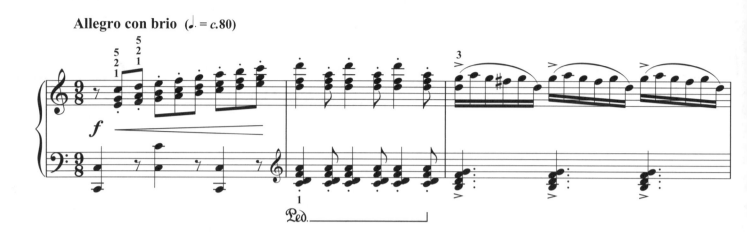

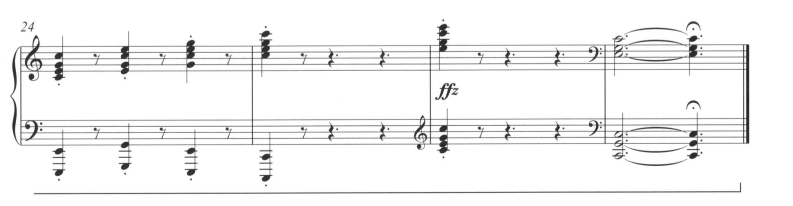

STUDY IN F MINOR

Op.30, No.16

Johann Baptist Cramer
(1771–1858)

STUDY IN F

No. 65 *from* Gradus ad Parnassum

Muzio Clementi
(1752–1832)

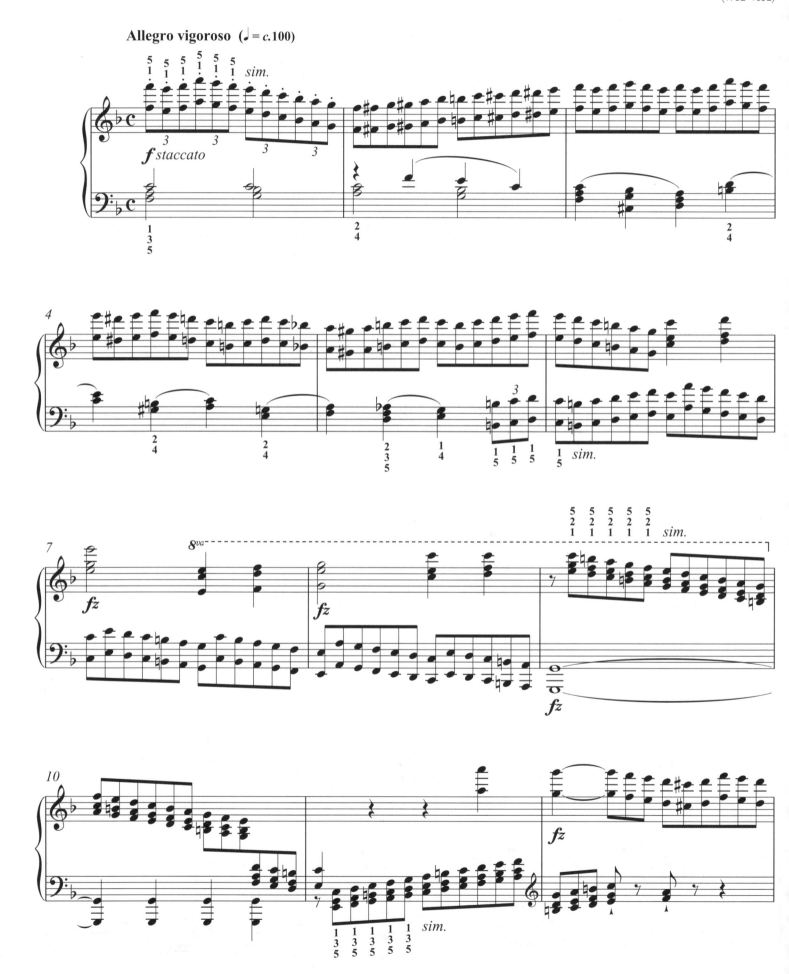

STUDY IN E
Op.45, No.9

Stephen Heller
(1813–1888)

STUDY IN A

No.9 *from* Gradus ad Parnassum

Muzio Clementi
(1752–1832)

STUDY IN D MINOR

Op.740, No.37

Carl Czerny
(1791–1857)

STUDY IN C SHARP MINOR

Op.2, No.1

Alexander Scriabin
(1872–1915)

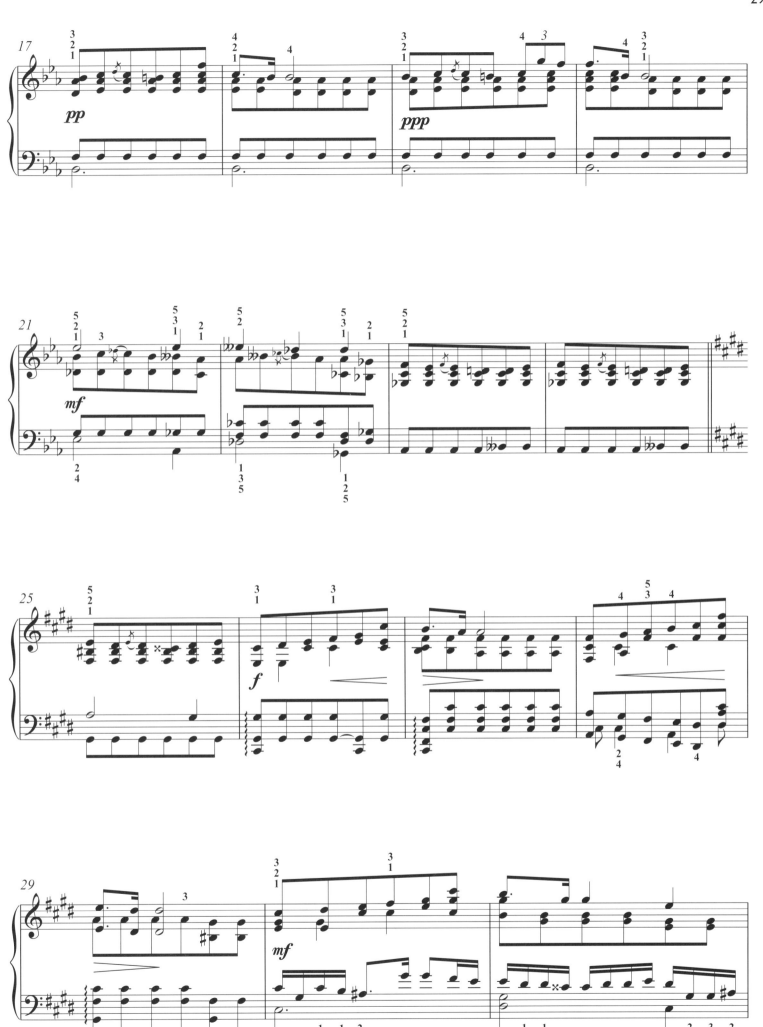

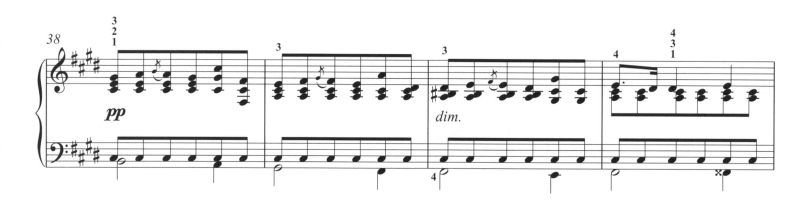

Real Repertoire Piano

Including pieces ranging from JS Bach's Invention in F *to Peter Maxwell Davies'* Farewell to Stromness

0-571-52119-3

Baroque Real Repertoire

Including JS Bach's Invention in A minor, *Purcell's* A New Ground *and Paradies'* Toccata

0-571-52333-1

Classical Real Repertoire

Including Beethoven's Bagatelles in D *and* E flat, *Hummel's* To Alexis *and*
Schubert's Moment Musical in F minor

0-571-52334-X

Romantic Real Repertoire

Including Chopin's Waltz in C sharp minor, *Field's* Nocturne in B flat *and*
Fauré's Romance sans paroles

0-571-52335-8

Twentieth Century Real Repertoire

Including Bartók's Melody in the Mist, *Debussy's* The Little Shepherd *and*
Sculthorpe's Evening Star *and* Singing Sun

0-571-52336-6

Christine Brown (editor)

To buy Faber Music publications or to find out about the full range of titles available
please contact your local music retailer or Faber Music sales enquiries:

Faber Music Ltd, Burnt Mill, Elizabeth Way, Harlow CM20 2HX
Tel: +44 (0) 1279 82 89 82   Fax: +44 (0) 1279 82 89 83
sales@fabermusic.com   fabermusic.com   expressprintmusic.com

For more in a chilled mood
try the rest of the series ...
each with a free Naxos CD

Adagio Chillout
Favourite slow movements and contemplative pieces,
including Beethoven's *Moonlight Sonata*,
Schumann's *Träumerei* and Mendelssohn's
Song without words '*Sweet Remembrance*'.

0-571-52435-4

Chill with Chopin
Including masterpieces such as the '*Raindrop*' Prelude,
the *March Funèbre* from Sonata in B flat minor, and
the Waltz in A flat '*L'Adieu*'.

0-571-52438-9

Chill with Mozart
The most beautiful movements by Mozart,
including the first movement from Sonata in C K.545,
the Fantasia in D minor K.397 and
Adagio in B minor K.540.

0-571-52436-2

Chill with Debussy
Unmissable favourites such as *Clair de lune*,
La fille aux cheveux de lin and *Arabesque* No.1.

0-571-52437-0

To buy Faber Music publications or to find out about the full range of titles available
please contact your local music retailer or Faber Music sales enquiries:

Faber Music Ltd, Burnt Mill, Elizabeth Way, Harlow CM20 2HX
Tel: +44 (0) 1279 82 89 82   Fax: +44 (0) 1279 82 89 83
sales@fabermusic.com   fabermusic.com   expressprintmusic.com